HEAD OVER HEELS

HEAD
···· *over* ····
HEELS

HOW TO FALL IN LOVE
and LAND ON YOUR FEET

DR. JAMES
DOBSON

Regal

From Gospel Light
Ventura, California, U.S.A.

Published by Regal
From Gospel Light
Ventura, California, U.S.A.
www.regalbooks.com
Printed in the U.S.A.

Library of Congress Cataloging-in-Publication Data
Dobson, James C., 1936-
Head over heels : how to fall in love and land on your feet /
James Dobson.
p. cm.
"Excerpted from 'Emotions, can you trust them?'
by Dr. James Dobson."
ISBN 978-0-8307-4714-6 (hard cover)
ISBN 978-0-8307-6138-8 (trade paper)
1. Love—Religious aspects—Christianity. 2. Man-woman relationships—
Religious aspects—Christianity. I. Dobson, James C., 1936-
Emotions, can you trust them? II. Title. III. Title:
How to fall in love and land on your feet.
BV4639.D535 2011
241'.6765—dc22
2011000867

Rights for publishing this book outside the U.S.A. or in on-English
languages are administered by Gospel Light Worldwide, an international
not-for-profit ministry. For additional information, please visit
www.glww.org, email info@glww.org, or write to Gospel Light Worldwide,
1957 Eastman Avenue, Ventura, CA 93003, U.S.A.

To order copies of this book and other Regal products in bulk quantities,
please contact us at 1-800-446-7735.

THIS BOOK IS AFFECTIONATELY
DEDICATED TO MY WIFE, SHIRLEY,
WITH WHOM I FELL "HEAD OVER HEELS"
MORE THAN 50 YEARS AGO.
I'VE SHARED THE GREATEST MOMENTS
OF MY LIFE WITH THIS FINE LADY,
AND I THANK GOD FOR BRINGING
HER INTO MY LIFE.

Contents

INTRODUCTION

You are about to read a book about one of the strongest and most misunderstood of all human emotions—romantic love. The topic of human emotions always reminds me of a story my mother told about the high school she attended in 1930. It was located in a small Oklahoma town that had produced a series of terrible football teams. They hadn't won a game in years. Understandably, the students and their parents were dispirited by the drubbing their team was given every Friday night. It must have been awful.

Finally, a wealthy oil producer decided to take matters in his own hands. He asked to speak to the team in the locker room after yet another devastating defeat. What followed was one of the most dramatic football speeches in the school's history. This businessman proceeded to offer a brand-new Ford to every boy on the team, and to each coach, if they would simply defeat their bitter rival in the next game. Notre Dame's great coach, Knute Rockne, couldn't have said it better.

The team howled and cheered and slapped each other on their padded behinds. At night they dreamed about touchdowns and rumble seats. The entire school caught the spirit of ecstasy, and a holiday fever pervaded the campus. Each player could visualize himself behind the wheel of a sleek coupe, with eight gorgeous girls hanging all over his adolescent body.

Finally, the big night arrived and the team assembled in the locker room. Excitement was at an unprecedented high. The coach made his own great speech, and the boys hurried out to face the enemy. They assembled on the sidelines, put their hands

Seven days of hoorah and whoop-de-do simply couldn't compensate for the players' lack of discipline, talent, conditioning, practice, coaching, drilling, experience and character. Such is the nature of human emotions. They can be unreliable, ephemeral and even a bit foolish.

together and shouted a simultaneous "Rah!" Then they ran onto the field . . . and were demolished, 38-0.

The team's exuberance did not translate into a single point on the scoreboard. Seven days of hoorah and whoop-de-do simply couldn't compensate for the players' lack of discipline, talent, conditioning, practice, coaching, drilling, experience and character.

Such is the nature of human emotions. They can be unreliable, ephemeral and even a bit foolish. The failure to understand how they work can lead to many painful mistakes. That is especially true of romantic love. It produces a wonderful feeling for a starry-eyed couple, but what does being "in love" really mean? Let's try to answer that question.

THE MEANING OF
ROMANTIC LOVE

Many young people grow up with a very distorted concept of romantic love. They confuse the real thing with infatuation, and they idealize marriage into something it can never be. To help clarify this misconception, I developed a brief "True or False" quiz for use in teaching groups of teenagers. But to my surprise, I found that adults didn't score much higher on the quiz than their adolescent offspring. You may want to take this quiz to measure your understanding of romance, love and marriage. A discussion of each True/False statement follows the quiz to help you discover for yourself the difference between distorted love and the real thing.

What Do You Believe About Love?

Check "True" or "False" for each of the statements on the following page.

True False

☐ | ☐ 1. "Love at first sight" occurs between some people.

☐ | ☐ 2. It is easy to distinguish real love from infatuation.

☐ | ☐ 3. People who sincerely love each other will not fight and argue.

☐ | ☐ 4. God selects *one* particular person for each of us to marry, and He will guide us together.

☐ | ☐ 5. If a man and woman genuinely love each other, then hardships and troubles will have little or no effect on their relationship.

☐ | ☐ 6. It is better to marry the wrong person than to remain single and lonely throughout life.

☐ | ☐ 7. It is not harmful or wrong to have sexual intercourse before marriage if the couple has a meaningful relationship.

☐ | ☐ 8. If a couple is genuinely in love, that condition is permanent—lasting a lifetime.

☐ | ☐ 9. A short courtship (six months or less) is best.

☐ | ☐ 10. Teenagers are more capable of genuine love than are older people.

Boy Meets Girl—Hooray for Love!

While there are undoubtedly some differences of opinion regarding the answers for the True/False quiz, I feel strongly about what I consider to be correct responses to each item. In fact, I believe that many of the common problems in marriage develop from a misunderstanding of one or more of these 10 items. Consider this example:

The confusion begins when boy meets girl and the entire sky lights up in romantic profusion. Smoke and fire are followed by lightning and thunder, and the dazzled couple finds itself knee deep in what may or may not be true love. Adrenaline is pumped into the cardiovascular system by the pint, and every nerve is charged with 220 volts of electricity. Then two little couriers go racing up the respective backbones of the boy and girl and blast their exhilarating messages into each spinning head: "This is it! The search is

*The confusion begins when boy meets
girl and the entire sky lights up in
romantic profusion. Smoke and fire are
followed by lightning and thunder, and the
dazzled couple finds itself knee deep
in what may or may not be true love.*

over! I've found the perfect human being! Hooray for love!"

For our romantic young couple, it is simply too wonderful to behold. They want to be together 24 hours a day—to take walks in the rain and sit by the fire and kiss and smooch and cuddle. They get all teary-eyed just thinking about each other. And it doesn't take long for the subject of marriage to propose itself. So they set the date and reserve the chapel and contact the minister and order the flowers.

The big night arrives amidst Mother's tears and Dad's grins, and jealous bridesmaids and frightened little flower girls. The candles are lit and the bride's sister butchers two beautiful songs. Then the vows are muttered, rings are placed on trembling fingers and the preacher tells the groom to kiss his new wife. Then they sprint up the aisle, each flashing 32 teeth, on the way to the reception.

Friends and well-wishers hug and kiss the bride and roll their eyes at the groom, eat the awful cake and follow the instructions of the perspiring photographer. Finally, the new Mr. and Mrs. run from the party in a flurry of birdseed and confetti and strike out on their honeymoon. So far the beautiful dream remains intact, but it is living on borrowed time.

Not only is the first night in the hotel less exciting than advertised—but it also turns into a comical disaster. She is exhausted and tense, and he is self-conscious and phony. From the beginning, sex is tinged with the threat of possible failure. Their vast expectations about the marital bed lead to disappointment and frustration and fear. Since most human beings have an almost neurotic desire to feel sexually adequate, each partner tends to blame his or her mate for any orgasmic problems, which eventually adds a note of anger and resentment to their relationship.

About 3 o'clock on the second afternoon, the new husband gives 10 minutes of thought to the fateful question, "Have I made an enormous mistake?" His silence increases her anxieties, and the seeds of disenchantment are born. Each partner has far too much time to think about the consequences of this new relationship, and they both begin to feel trapped.

Their initial argument is a silly thing. They struggle momentarily over how much money to spend for dinner on the third night of the honeymoon. She wants to go someplace romantic to charge up the atmosphere, and he wants to eat with Ronald McDonald. The flare-up lasts only a few moments and is followed by apologies, but some harsh words have been exchanged, which took the keen edge off the beautiful dream. They will soon learn to hurt each other more effectively.

Somehow, they make it through the six-day trip and travel home to set up house-keeping together. Then the world starts to splinter and disintegrate before their eyes. The next fight is bigger and better than the first; he leaves home for two hours and she calls her mother.

Throughout the first year, they are engaged in a recurring contest of wills, each vying for power and leadership. And in the midst of this tug-of-war, she staggers out of the obstetrician's office with the words ringing in her ears, "I have some good news for you, Mrs. Jones!" If there is anything on earth Mrs. Jones doesn't need right now, it is "good news" from an obstetrician.

From there to the final conflict, we see two disappointed, confused and deeply hurt young people, wondering how it all came about. A little tow-headed lad or a beautiful little princess soon comes into the family.

That child and those yet to come may never enjoy the benefits of a stable home. He'll be raised by his mother and will always wonder, *"Why doesn't Dad live here anymore?"*

The picture I have painted does not reflect every young marriage, obviously, but it is representative of far too many of them. The divorce rate is higher in America than in any other civilized nation in the world, and it is rising. In the case of our disillusioned young couple, what happened to their romantic dream? How did the relationship that began with such enthusiasm turn so quickly into hatred and hostility? They could not have been more enamored with each other at the beginning, but their "happiness" blew up in their startled faces. Why didn't it last? How can others avoid the same unpleasant surprise?

Perhaps our True/False quiz will provide some answers.

BELIEFS
ABOUT LOVE

Here are the answers to our quiz:

ITEM 1

"Love at first sight" occurs between some people.

False. Though some readers will disagree with me, love at first sight is a physical and emotional impossibility. Why? Because love is not simply a feeling of romantic excitement; it goes beyond intense sexual attraction; it exceeds the thrill at having "captured" a highly desirable social prize. These are emotions that are unleashed at first sight, but they *do not constitute love*. I wish every young couple knew that fact. These temporary feelings differ from love in that they place the spotlight on the one experiencing them. "What is happening to *me*? This is the most fantastic thing *I've* ever been through! I think I am in love!"

You see, these emotions are selfish in the sense that they are motivated by a person's own gratification. They have little to do with the new lover.

Such a person has not fallen in love with another person; *he or she has fallen in love with love!* And there is an enormous difference between the two.

Pop songs, which are many teenagers' primary source of information about love, reveal a vast ignorance of the topic. This is just as relevant to today's music as it was in years gone by. One immortal number from yesteryear asserts, "Before the dance was through, I knew I was in love with you." I wonder if the crooner was quite so confident the next morning. Another confessed, "I didn't know just what to do, so I whispered 'I love you!'" That one still gets to me.

The idea of basing a lifetime commitment on teenage confusion seems a bit shaky at best.

The Partridge Family recorded a song years ago that also betrayed a lack of understanding of real love; it said, "I woke up in love today 'cause I went to sleep with you on my mind." Love in this sense is nothing more than a frame of mind—and it's just about that permanent. Finally, a rock group from the '60s called *The Doors* took the prize for the most ignorant musical number of the twentieth century; the chorus ran, "Hello, I love you, won't you tell me your name!"

Did you know that the idea of marriage based on romantic affection is a rather recent development in human affairs? Prior to A.D. 1200, in the Western world the families of the bride and groom arranged the weddings, and it never occurred to anyone that they were supposed to "fall in love." In fact, the concept of romantic love was actually popularized by

William Shakespeare. There are times when
I wish the old Englishman was here to help
us figure out what he had in mind.

Here's my best explanation: Real love, in
contrast to popular notions, is an expression
of the deepest appreciation for another human being; it is an intense awareness of his
or her needs and longings for the past, present and future. It is unselfish and giving and
caring. And believe me, these are not atti-
tudes one "falls" into at first sight, as though
he or she were tumbling into a ditch.

I have developed a lifelong love for my
wife, Shirley, but it was not something I fell
into. I *grew* into it, and that process took
time. I had to know her before I could ap-
preciate the depth and stability of her character—to become acquainted with the nuances
of her personality, which I now cherish. The
familiarity from which love has blossomed
simply could not be generated on "some

enchanted evening . . . across a crowded room" (as another old crooner would have it). One cannot love an unknown object, regardless of how attractive or sexy or nubile it is!

ITEM 2

It is easy to distinguish real love from infatuation.

Again, this statement is false. That wild ride at the start of a romantic adventure bears all the earmarks of a lifetime trip. Just try to tell a 16-year-old dreamer that he is not really in love—that he's merely infatuated. He'll whip out his guitar and sing you a song about "true love." He knows what he feels, and he feels great. But he'd better enjoy the rollercoaster ride while it lasts, because it has a predictable end point.

I must stress this fact with the greatest emphasis: The exhilaration of infatuation is *never* a permanent condition. Period! If you expect to live on the top of that mountain year after year, you can forget it! Emotions swing from high to low to high in cyclical rhythm; and because romantic excitement is an emotion, it too will certainly oscillate. If the thrill of sexual encounter is identified as genuine love, then disillusionment and disappointment are already knocking at the door.

How many vulnerable young couples "fall in love with love" on the first date and lock themselves into marriage before the natural swing of their emotions has even progressed through the first dip? Then they awaken one morning without that neat feeling and conclude that love has died. In reality, it was never there in the first place. They were fooled by an emotional "high."

I was trying to explain this up-and-down characteristic of our psychological nature to

How many vulnerable young couples "fall in love with love" on the first date—and lock themselves into marriage before the natural swing of their emotions has even progressed through the first dip?

a group of 100 young married couples. During the discussion period, someone asked a young man in the group why he got married so young, and he replied, " 'Cause I didn't know 'bout that wiggly line until it was too late!" Alas, that wiggly line has trapped more than one young romanticist.

The "wiggly line" is manipulated up and down by the circumstances of life. Even when a man and woman love each other deeply and genuinely, they will find themselves supercharged on one occasion and emotionally bland on another. You see, their love is not defined by the highs and lows, but it is dependent *on a commitment of their will.* Stability comes from this irrepressible determination to make a success of marriage and to keep the flame aglow *regardless of the circumstances.*

Unfortunately, not everyone agrees with the divinely inspired concept of permanent marriage. The late anthropologist Dr. Margaret Mead advocated trial marriage for the young. She and other writers have encouraged young people to accept communal marriage and contract marriage and cohabitation. Even our music has reflected our aimless groping for an innovative relationship between men and women.

One such idea is that romantic love can only survive in the *absence* of permanent commitment. Singer Glen Campbell translated this thought into music in his once-popular song titled "Gentle on My Mind." Paraphrasing the lyrics, he said it was not the ink-stained signatures dried on some marriage certificate that kept his bedroll stashed behind the couch in his lover's home; it was knowing that he could get up and leave her anytime he wished—that she had no hooks into his hide. It was the freedom to abandon her that kept her "gentle on [his] mind."

What a ridiculous notion to think a woman exists who could let her lover come and go with no feelings of loss, rejection or abandonment! How ignorant it is of the power of love (and sex) to make us "one flesh," inevitably ripping and tearing that flesh at the time of separation.

And, of course, Glen Campbell's song said nothing about the little children who are born from such a relationship, each one wondering if Daddy will be there tomorrow morning, if he will help them pay their bills, or if he will be out by a railroad track somewhere, sipping coffee from a tin can and thinking the good thoughts in the backroads of his mind. Can't you see his little woman standing with her children in the front doorway, waving a hanky and calling, "Good-bye, Dear. Drop in when you can"?

Let's return to the question before us: If genuine love is rooted in a commitment of the will, how can one know when it arrives? How can it be distinguished from temporary infatuation? How can the feeling be interpreted if it is unreliable and inconstant?

There is only one answer to those questions: *It takes time*. The best advice I can give a couple contemplating marriage (or any other important decision) is this: Make *no* important, life-shaping decisions quickly or impulsively; and when in doubt, stall for time. That's not a bad suggestion for all of us to apply.

ITEM 3

People who sincerely love each other will not fight and argue.

I doubt if this third item actually requires an answer. Some marital conflict is as inevitable as the sunrise, even in loving marriages. There is a difference, however, between healthy and unhealthy combat, depending on the way the

*The best advice I can give a couple
contemplating marriage (or any other
important decision) is this: Make no important,
life-shaping decisions quickly or impulsively;
and when in doubt, stall for time. That's not a
bad suggestion for all of us to apply.*

disagreement is handled. In an unstable marriage, anger is usually hurled directly at the
partner. Hostile, person-centered "you messages" strike at the heart of one's self-worth
and produce intense internal upheaval:

"You never do anything right!"
"Why did I ever marry you?"
"How can you be so stupid (or un-
    reasonable or unfair)?"
"You are getting more like your
    mother every day."

The wounded partner often responds in
like manner, hurling back hateful remarks
punctuated with tears and profanity. The
avowed purpose of this kind of infighting is
to hurt, and it is very effective. The cutting
words will never be forgotten, even though
uttered in a moment of irrational anger.
Such combat is not only unhealthy but also

vicious and corrosive. It erodes the marriage relationship and can easily destroy it.

Healthy conflict, on the other hand, remains focused on the issue around which the disagreement began. Issue-centered "I" messages let your partner know what is wrong and that he or she is not the main target:

"I'm worried about all of these bills."
"I get upset when I don't know you
     will be late for dinner."
"I was embarrassed by what you said at
     the party last night—I felt foolish."

Any area of struggle—worry, anger, embarrassment—can be emotional and tense, but it can be much less damaging to the egos of both spouses if they will focus on the basic disagreement and try to resolve it together. A healthy couple can work through problems by compromise and negotiation. There will

Head Over Heels

still be pain and hurt, but a husband and wife will have fewer embedded barbs to pluck out the following morning. The ability to fight *properly* may be the most important skill to be learned by newlyweds.

Those who never comprehend the technique are usually left with two alternatives: (1) turn the anger and resentment inward in silence, where it will fester and accumulate through the years, or (2) blast away at the personhood of one's mate. The divorce courts are well represented by couples in both categories.[1]

ITEM 4

God selects *one* particular person for each of us to marry, and He will guide us together.

A young man whom I was counseling once told me that he awoke in the middle of the night with the strong impression that God

38

wanted him to marry a young lady whom he had dated casually only a few times. They were not even going together at that time and hardly knew each other. The next morning he called her and relayed the message that God had supposedly sent him during the night. The girl figured she shouldn't argue with God, so she accepted the proposal. They have now been married for seven years and have struggled for survival since their wedding day!

Anyone who believes that God guarantees a successful marriage to every Christian is in for a shock. This is not to say that He is disinterested in the choice of a mate, or that He will not answer a specific request for guidance on this all-important decision. Certainly, His will should be sought in such a critical matter. I consulted Him repeatedly before proposing to my wife.

However, I do not believe that God performs a routine matchmaking service for

*I do not believe that God performs
a routine matchmaking service for everyone
who worships Him. He has given us
judgment, common sense and discretionary
powers, and He expects us to exercise these
abilities in matters matrimonial.*

everyone who worships Him. He has given us judgment, common sense and discretionary powers, and He expects us to exercise these abilities in matters matrimonial. Those who believe otherwise are likely to enter marriage glibly, thinking, *God would have stopped us if He didn't approve*. To such confident people I can only say, "Lotsa luck."

ITEM 5

If a man and woman genuinely love each other, then hardships and troubles will have little or no effect on their relationship.

Another common misconception about the meaning of "true love" is that it is impervious to the stresses of life and that it stands like the rock of Gibraltar during hard times. Sometimes, love does not conquer all. The Beatles endorsed this notion with their song, "All we need is love, love, love is all we need." Unfortunately, we need a bit more.

I served on the attending staff for Children's Hospital of Los Angeles for 14 years. We saw numerous children with genetic and metabolic problems throughout the years, most of which involved mental and physical disabilities in our young patients. The emotional impact of such diagnoses on the families was devastating. Even in stable, loving marriages, the guilt and disappointment of having produced a "broken" child often drove a wedge between the distressed mother and father. In a similar manner, the fiber of love can be weakened by financial hardships, disease, business setbacks or prolonged separation. In short, we must conclude that love is vulnerable to pain and trauma, and often wobbles when assaulted by life. It must be protected or nurtured when the hard times come.

ITEM 6

It is better to marry the wrong person than to remain single and lonely throughout life.

Again, the answer is false. Generally speaking, it is less painful to be searching for an end to loneliness than to be embroiled in the emotional turmoil of a bad marriage. Yet the threat of being forever single causes many young women, especially, to grab the first train that rambles down the marital track. And too often it offers a one-way ticket to trouble.

The fear of never finding a mate can cause a single person to ignore his or her better judgment and compromise his or her standards. A young woman may argue with herself in this manner: *John isn't a Christian, but maybe I can influence him after we're married. He drinks too much, but that's probably because he's young and carefree. And we don't have much in common, but I'm sure we'll learn to love each other more as time passes. Besides, what could be worse than living alone?*

This kind of rationalization is based on a desperate hope for a matrimonial miracle, but storybook endings are uncommon events in everyday life. When one plunges into marriage despite the obvious warning flags, both the husband and wife are gambling with their remaining years.

For readers who are single today, *please* believe me when I say that a bad marriage can be one of the most miserable experiences on earth! It often leads to rejection, hurt feelings, wounded children and sleepless nights. Certainly, a solitary journey as a single person can be a meaningful and fulfilling life. At least, it does not involve "a house divided against itself" (Mark 3:25).

*When one plunges into marriage
despite the obvious warning flags, both the
husband and wife are gambling with
their remaining years. For readers who are
single today, please believe me when I say that
a bad marriage can be one of the
most miserable experiences on earth!*

ITEM 7

It is not harmful or wrong to have sexual intercourse before marriage if the couple has a meaningful relationship.

This item represents *the* most dangerous of the popular misconceptions about romantic love, not only for individuals but also for our nation. During the past several decades we have witnessed the tragic disintegration of sexual mores and traditional concepts of morality. Responding to a steady onslaught by the entertainment industry and by the media, many people have begun to believe that premarital intercourse is healthy and morally acceptable. These views reflect the sexual vacuity of the age in which we live.

It is unusual for social scientists to be in virtual unanimity regarding the issues they are studying, but most are in agreement about the consequences of early sexual behavior. It is often the first step toward devastating emotional and physical harm, especially among those for whom intercourse has become habitual.

As I state in my book *Bringing Up Girls*, it is almost impossible to overstate the scope of this problem. About 19 million new cases of STDs occur each year among all age groups in the United States.[2] Those who "sleep around," even occasionally, will inevitably—and I do mean inevitably—be infected with a sexually transmitted illness (or an array of them). Condoms may reduce the risk, but they are problematic too. They slip, they break, they leak and they become brittle with age. In some instances, all it takes to contract a fine case of syphilis or gonorrhea or chlamydia or herpes or another of the 30 common STDs is to make a single mistake with a carrier. The chances of becoming infected by an infected partner are as high as 40 percent per encounter.[3]

One of the dreaded diseases mentioned above is the human papillomavirus, or HPV, which deserves special attention. The Centers for Disease Control and Prevention estimate that 19 million people are infected annually with this disease.[4] At least 50 percent of sexually active individuals will acquire HPV during their lives.[5] By 50 years of age, 80 percent of women will acquire a genital HPV infection.[6] There are more than 100 strains of this infection, 40 strains of which affect the genital area. Some of them cause cancer of the cervix.[7] Most people do not realize they are infected or that they are passing the virus to a sex partner. Women who contract one of these diseases will need medical evaluation regularly and may require special testing and treatment procedures.

Other studies indicate that oral sex among teens between ages 15 and 19 is more common than sexual intercourse.[8] Seventy percent of those between 17 and 19 say that they have had oral sex.[9] Unbelievably, most teens view that activity as casual and non-intimate.[10] Some of them apparently choose oral sex instead of intercourse to retain their "virginal status" and to prevent disease.[11] What they don't know is that many of the sexually transmitted organisms they bring home, such as herpes and other viruses, are incurable even though they are treatable. Strains of the human papillomavirus can cause mouth and throat cancer and are spread by oral sexual activity. Those are the cold, hard facts.

Dr. Joel Ernster, an otolaryngologist who practices in Colorado Springs, Colorado, wrote, "Oral sex has implications that are way beyond what we first thought."[12] He said that married men with families who engaged in this sexual activity decades ago can still be carrying the infection.

In study after study, we are seeing confirmation of what many of us have known for 20 years but still seems to be a secret among most teens and young adults: There is no such thing as safe sex. U.S. health officials estimated in 2007 that one-quarter of all women in this country between 14 and 59 are infected with a virus that causes warts and most cases of cervical cancer.[13] Does that shock you as much as it does me? Twenty-five percent of the female teens, wives, sisters, aunts and some grandmothers that you see walking around carry this disease. Some will die from cancers resulting from HPV. These epidemics of sexually transmitted diseases are swirling all around us.

Indiscriminate sexual activity not only represents an individual threat to survival,

In study after study, we are seeing confirmation of what many of us have known for 20 years but still seems to be a secret among most teens and young adults: There is no such thing as safe sex. The epidemics of sexually transmitted diseases are swirling all around us.

but it has major implications for nations too. Anthropologist J. D. Unwin conducted an exhaustive study of the 88 civilizations that have existed in the history of the world. Each culture has reflected a similar life cycle, beginning with a strict code of sexual conduct and ending with the demand for complete "freedom" to express individual passion. Unwin reports that *every* society that endorsed sexual promiscuity was soon to perish. There have been no exceptions.[14]

Why do you suppose the reproductive urge within us is so relevant to cultural survival? It is because the energy that holds societies together is sexual in nature! The physical attraction between men and women causes them to establish families and to invest themselves in their development. It encourages them to work and save and toil to ensure their survival. Their sexual energy provides the impetus for the raising of healthy children and for the transfer of values from one generation to the next.

Sexual drives urge a man to work when he would rather play. They cause a woman to save when she would rather spend. In short, the sexual aspect of our nature—when released exclusively within the family—produces stability and responsibility that would not otherwise occur. When a nation is composed of millions of devoted, responsible family units, the entire society is stable, responsible and resilient.

If sexual energy within the family is the key to a healthy society, then its release outside those boundaries is potentially catastrophic. The very force that binds a people together then becomes the agent for its own destruction.

Perhaps this point can be illustrated by an analogy between sexual energy in the nuclear family and physical energy in the nucleus of a tiny atom. Electrons, neutrons and protons are held in delicate balance by an electrical force within each atom. But when that atom and its neighbors are split in nuclear fission (such as in a nuclear bomb), the energy that had provided the internal stability is then released with shocking power and destruction. There is ample reason to believe that this comparison between the nucleus of the atom and the nuclear family is more than incidental.

Who can deny that a society is seriously weakened when the intense sexual urge between men and women becomes an instrument for suspicion and intrigue within millions of individual families? Under those circumstances, a woman never knows what her husband is doing when he is away from home, and a husband can't trust his wife in his absence. When these sexual urges go unchecked, as they often do, we end up with half of all brides pregnant at the altar, and newlyweds who have lost the exclusive wonder of the marital bed.

Unfortunately, the saddest victim of an immoral society of this nature is the vulnerable child who hears his parents fighting and arguing. Their tensions and frustrations spill over into his world, and the instability of his home leaves its ugly scars on his young mind. Then he watches his parents separate in anger, and he often says goodbye to the father he needs and loves.

Or perhaps we should speak of the thousands of babies born to unmarried teenage mothers each year—many of whom will never know the safety of a warm, nurturing home. Or maybe we should discuss the rampant scourge of venereal disease, including the deadly AIDS virus, which has reached epidemic proportions.

Illegitimate births, abortions, disease, even death—this is the true vomitus of the sexual revolution, and I am tired of hearing it romanticized and glorified. God has clearly forbidden irresponsible sexual behavior—not to deprive us of fun and pleasure, but to spare us the consequences of this festering way of life.

ITEM 8

If a couple is genuinely in love, that condition is permanent— lasting a lifetime.

Love, even genuine love, is a fragile thing. Let me say it again: A marital relationship must be maintained and protected if it is to survive. Love can perish when a husband or wife works seven days a week, when there is no time for romantic activity, when the man and woman forget how to talk to each other.

The keen edge in a loving relationship may be dulled through the routine pressures of living, as I experienced during the early days of my marriage to Shirley. I was working full time and trying to finish my doctorate at the University of Southern California. My wife was teaching school and maintaining our small home. I remember clearly the evening when I realized what this busy life was doing to our relationship. We still loved each other, but it had been too long since we had felt a spirit of warmth and closeness. My textbooks were pushed aside that night and we went for a long walk. The following semester, I carried a very light load in school and postponed my academic goals so as to preserve that which I valued more highly. I returned to my studies the next semester.

Where does your marriage rank on your hierarchy of values? Does it get the leftovers and scraps from your busy schedule, or is it something of great worth to be preserved and supported? It can die if left untended.

ITEM 9

A short courtship
(six months or less) is best.

The answer to this question is incorporated in the reply to the second item regarding infatuation. Short courtships reflect impulsive decisions about lifetime commitments, and they are risky business, at best.

ITEM 10

Teenagers are more capable of
genuine love than are older people.

If this item were true, then we would be hard pressed to explain why approximately half of teenage marriages end in divorce in the first few years. To the contrary, the kind of love that I have been describing—unselfish, giving, caring commitment—requires a measure of maturity to make it work. And maturity is a developing thing in most teen-agers. Adolescent romance is an exciting part of growing up, but it seldom meets the criteria for the deeper relationships of which successful marriages are composed.

Notes

1. For more information on how to handle conflict in a healthy way, read David Augsburger, *Caring Enough to Confront* (Ventura, CA: Regal Books, 2009).
2. "Sexually Transmitted Disease Surveillance, 2007," Centers for Disease Control and Prevention. The full report is available at http://www.cdc.gov/std/stats07.
3. E. Johannisson, "STDs, AIDS and Reproductive Health," *Advances in Contraception*, June 2005.
4. "Genital HPV Infection: CDC Fact Sheet, 2009." See http://www.cdc.gov/STD/HPV/STDFact-HPV.htm.
5. Ibid.
6. Ibid.
7. Ibid.
8. Laura Duberstein Lindberg, Rachel Jones and John S. Santelli, "Non-Coital Sexual Activities Among Adolescents," *Journal of Adolescent Health,* September 2008, pp. 231-238.
9. Laura Sessions Stepp, "Study: Half of All Teens Have Had Oral Sex," *Washington Post,* September 16, 2005, National Center for Health Statistics, 2005.
10. Teen Sex Survey conducted by Princeton Survey Research Associates International, 2004. See http://www.msnbc.msn.com/id/6839072.
11. Ibid., *Contraceptive Technology Update* 22, no. 5 (May 2001).
12. "Studies Tie Oral Sex to Throat Cancer in Some Men," *Colorado Springs Gazette,* October 22, 2007.
13 "Sexually Transmitted Disease Surveillance, 2007."
14. Joseph Daniel Unwin, "Sexual Regulations and Cultural Behavior," address given on March 27, 1935, to the medical section of the *British Psychological Society*, printed by Oxford University Press (London, England).

LIFELONG
COMMITMENT

All 10 items on the brief questionnaire are false, for they represent the 10 most common misconceptions about the meaning of romantic love. Sometimes I wish the test could be used as a basis for issuing marriage licenses: Those scoring 9 or 10 would qualify with honor; those getting 5 to 8 items right would be required to wait an extra six months before marriage; those confused dreamers answering 4 or fewer items correctly would be recommended for permanent celibacy! (Seriously, what we probably need is a cram-course for everyone contemplating wedding bells.)

I want to share the words I wrote to my wife on an anniversary card on our eighth anniversary. What I said to her may not be expressed in the way you would communicate with your mate. I do hope, however, that my words illustrate the genuine, uncompromising love that I have been describing:

To My Darlin' Wife, Shirley
on the occasion of our Eighth Anniversary

I'm sure you remember the many occasions during our eight years of marriage when the tide of love and affection soared high above the crest—times when our feeling for each other was almost limitless. This kind of intense emotion can't be brought about voluntarily, but it often accompanies a time of particular happiness. We felt it when I was offered my first professional position. We felt it when the world's most precious child came home from the maternity ward of Huntington Hospital. We felt it when the University of Southern California chose to award a Ph.D. to me, and at other exciting times in our marital life. But emotions are strange! We felt the same closeness when the opposite kind of event took place; when threat and sadness entered our lives. We felt an intense closeness when a medical problem threatened to postpone our marriage plans. We felt it when you were hospitalized last year. I felt it intensely when I knelt over your unconscious form after a grinding automobile accident.

I'm trying to say this: Both happiness and threat bring that overwhelming appreciation and affection for a person's beloved sweetheart. But the fact is, day-to-day living is neither sorrowful nor exhilarating. Rather, it is composed of the routine, calm, everyday events in which we participate. And during these times, I enjoy the quiet, serene love that actually surpasses the effervescent display, in many ways. It is not as exuberant, perhaps, but it runs deep and solid. I find myself firmly in that kind of love on this Eighth Anniversary. Today I feel the steady and quiet affection that comes from a devoted heart. I am committed to you and your happiness, now more than I've ever been. I want to remain your "sweetheart."

When events throw us together emotionally, we will enjoy the thrill and romantic excitement. But during life's routine, like today, my love stands undiminished. Happy Anniversary to my wonderful wife.

Jim

The key phrase in my note to Shirley is, "I am committed to you." My love for my wife is not blown back and forth by the winds of change, by circumstances and environmental influences. Even though my fickle emotions jump from one extreme to another, my commitment remains solidly anchored. My love for my wife is sustained by an uncompromising determination to make it succeed.

*My love for my wife is not blown back
and forth by the winds of change,
by circumstances and environmental
influences. Even though my fickle emotions
jump from one extreme to another,
my commitment remains solidly anchored.
My love for my wife is sustained
by an uncompromising determination
to make it succeed.*

The essential investment of commitment is sorely missing in so many modern marriages. "I love you," they seem to say, "as long as I feel attracted to you, or as long as someone else doesn't look better, or as long as it is to my advantage to continue the relationship." Sooner or later, this unanchored love will certainly vaporize.

"For better or worse, for richer, for poorer, in sickness and in health, to love and to cherish, till death us do part . . ." That familiar pledge from the past still offers the most solid foundation upon which to build a marriage, for therein lies the real meaning of genuine romantic love.

By the way, my wife, Shirley, and I celebrated our fiftieth wedding anniversary in 2010. It is the most significant "accomplishment" of our lives. And I think it's going to work.

CONCLUSION

At the risk of redundancy, let me address the issue of romantic love for those who appear to be moving toward marriage. If you are that person, I urge you to make the decision to marry with great caution and much prayer. Think carefully about how well you know the individual to whom you are attracted. Ask yourself if he or she harbors addictive or behavioral quirks that may have been hidden from you until now, such as alcoholism, gambling, pornography, homosexual or lesbian leanings, other evidence of sexual immorality, lying and deceit, selfishness, a violent temper, physical or emotional abuse, uncleanness, financial mismanagement, mental illness, laziness, disinterest in spiritual matters, dislike of children, and hundreds of other characteristics that can wreak havoc on a relationship. These problems can and often do crop up after marriage, which sometimes take the other partner completely by surprise. The person you are convinced is the perfect human being may bring you nothing but sorrow and heartache for the rest of your life. I am sorry to throw cold water on what seems like the most wonderful experience of a romantic relationship, but I owe it to you to pose the tough questions.

Given the significance of a marital commitment, it seems incredibly foolish for a man or woman to become linked for life with someone he or she hardly knows. That is one of the most risky decisions a person can make. Simply "feeling" good about him or her is not sufficient. That great feeling that drives you can evaporate in a weekend.

Returning to the point made earlier, impressions are notoriously unreliable; they are often motivated by sexual attraction, loneliness, yearning, hope, the "gonging of Big Ben" and the need for love. All of these factors are legitimate and reasonable, but they can also lead to self-delusion. Millions of people have been so smitten by these desires that they ran past all the red flags. So what is a person to do with the ache inside? Marriage is one of the most marvelous gifts to us from the hand of our Creator, and matrimony should not be avoided just because it carries risks. Instead, there are good ways to test one's impressions to see whether they are valid or dangerous imposters.

Let me pose the following three questions that a person can consider to determine if he or she is doing the right thing, not only in regard to marriage, but also in respecting all major decisions in life. Stated another way, you can put your impressions to the test by asking yourself these questions:

1. Is It Scriptural?

You'll find specific answers to life's problems in the Word of God. Every expression of God's will conforms to His universal principles. If a

*Marriage is one of the most marvelous gifts
to us from the hand of our Creator,
and matrimony should not be avoided just
because it carries risks. Instead, there are good
ways to test one's impressions to see whether
they are valid or dangerous imposters.*

behavior is prohibited in the Bible, it can't be right. You can find relevant passages about the decision you are facing, not by random proof-texting, where you take a verse or two out of context to support a particular desire, but by studying relevant verses using a Bible concordance or computer software that offers a variety of interactive concordances, lexicons and commentaries. You will be surprised by how Scripture "talks" to you when you are genuinely seeking God's wisdom.

Without a standard of behavior against which to judge rightness or wrongness, we are in danger of making enormous mistakes with life's most important decisions. Most of us are very skilled at self-justification, especially when we want to do something badly enough. Perhaps the most striking example of this self-delusion I've seen occurred with a young couple that decided to engage in sexual intercourse before marriage. They had been raised in a church community, however, and had to deal with the problem of guilt. Thus, they actually got down on their knees and prayed about what they were about to do, and felt that the Lord assured them it was okay to proceed. And so they did, but knew intuitively that they had violated specific Scriptures.

Let the Word guide your decisions, not some feeling that bubbles up during the night. We are told in Scripture that Satan comes to us as "an angel of light" (2 Cor. 11:14). That means he counterfeits the work of the Holy Spirit. He has earned his reputation as the "father of lies" (John 8:44). Some of that deception is expressed in the form of impressions about romantic love.

2. Is It "Right"?"

Some things that we want to do are not specifically prohibited in Scripture, but common sense tells us that they are wrong.

Let the Word guide your decisions, not some feeling that bubbles up during the night. Satan counterfeits the work of the Holy Spirit. Some of that deception is expressed in the form of impressions about romantic love.

I am acquainted with another family that was damaged irreparably by the mother's impression to do something that I think was clearly wrong. Although she had three little children in the home, she felt that she was "called" to leave them to pursue another line of work. On very short notice, she left her kids in the care of a father who had no interest in caring for them. He worked six and seven days a week, and the children were left to fend for themselves.

The consequences were devastating. The youngest boy in the family lay awake at night, crying for his mommy. The older children had to assume adult responsibilities, which they were ill prepared to handle. There was no one at home to train and love and guide the development of this pitiful little family. I don't believe the mother's impression was from God, because it was neither scriptural nor right. I suspect she had other motives for fleeing her home, and she covered them by coming up with a noble explanation.

If you love someone, especially a husband or wife, you will try to do the right thing.

3. Is It Providential?

I have found it helpful in making critical decisions to watch the unfolding of circumstances and events around me. After praying, I pay attention to the doors that open and close, or to things occurring routinely that relate to the issue at hand. God is fully capable of letting His will be known to those who are watching and listening. Sometimes He speaks with whispered words, but at other times He nudges us with influential circumstances. Could they confirm that a relationship between a man and woman has the blessing of the Lord? I think so. You'll have to answer for yourself.

The point is that there are better ways to examine the meaning of love and to decide what to do about it. Interpreting what you feel may not be the most reliable method. Regardless of how you go about making this critically important decision, the strongest advice I would offer is to *give the matter time*. Impulsive, quick acts are likely to be regretted.

A Personal
Postscript

During a Marriage Encounter weekend in 1981, I wrote a letter to my wife, Shirley. Here is a portion of that letter (minus some introductory intimacies), which, I believe, illustrates the depth and intensity of genuine, lifelong romantic love.

> Who else shares the memory of my youth during which the foundations of love were laid? I ask you, who else could occupy the place that is reserved for the only woman who was *there* when I graduated from college and went to the Army and returned as a student at USC and bought my first decent car (and promptly wrecked it) and picked out an inexpensive wedding ring with you (and paid for it with Savings Bonds) and we prayed and thanked God for what we had.

Then we said the wedding vows, and my dad prayed, "Lord, You gave us Jimmy and Shirley as infants to love and cherish and raise for a season, and tonight, we give them back to You after our labor of love—not as two separate individuals, but as one!" And everyone cried.

Then we left for the honeymoon and spent all our money and came home to an apartment full of rice and a bell on the bed, and we had only just begun. You taught the second grade, and I taught (and fell in love with) a bunch of sixth graders and especially a kid named Norbert; and I earned a master's degree and passed the comprehensive exams for a doctorate; and we bought our first little home and remodeled it, and I dug up all the grass and buried it in a 10-foot hole that later sank and looked like two graves in the front yard—and while spreading the dirt to make a new lawn, I accidentally "planted" eight million ash seeds from our tree and discovered two weeks later that we had a forest growing between our house and the street.

Then, alas, you delivered our very own baby, and we loved her half to death and named her Danae Ann, and built a room on our little bungalow and gradually filled it with furniture. Then I joined the staff of Children's Hospital, and I did well there, but still didn't have enough money to pay our USC tuition and other expenses. So we sold (and ate) a Volkswagen. Then I earned a Ph.D., and we cried and thanked God for what we had.

In 1970, we brought home a little boy and named him James Ryan, and loved him half to death and didn't sleep for six months. And I labored over a manuscript titled *Dare to . . .* something or other and then reeled backward under a flood of favorable responses and a few not so favorable responses and received a small royalty check and thought it was a fortune, and I joined the faculty at USC School of Medicine and did well there.

Soon I found myself pacing the halls of Huntington Memorial Hospital as a team of grim-faced neurologists examined your nervous system for evidence of hypothalamic tumor, and I prayed and begged God to let me complete my life with my best friend, and He finally said, "Yes . . .

for now," and we cried and thanked Him for what we had.

And we bought a new house and promptly tore it to shreds and went skiing in Vail, Colorado, and tore your leg to shreds, and I called your mom to report the accident, and she tore me to shreds and our toddler, Ryan, tore the whole town of Arcadia to shreds. And the construction on the house seemed to go on forever, and you stood in the shattered living room and cried every Saturday night because so little had been accomplished. Then, during the worst of the mess, 100 friends gave us a surprise housewarming, and they slopped through the debris and mud and sawdust and cereal bowls and sandwich parts—and the next morning you groaned and asked, "Did it really happen?"

And I published a new book called *Hide or Seek* (What?) and everyone called it Hide *and* Seek, and the publisher sent us to Hawaii, and we stood on the balcony overlooking the bay and thanked God for what we had. Then I published *What Wives Wish,* and people liked it and the honors rolled in and the speaking requests arrived by the hundreds. Then you underwent risky surgery, and I said, "Lord, not now!" And the doctor said, "No cancer!" and we cried and thanked God for what we had.

Then I started a radio program and took a leave of absence from Children's Hospital and opened a little office in Arcadia called Focus on the Family, which a three-year-old radio listener later called "Poke us in the Fanny," and we got more visible. Then we went to Kansas City for a family vacation, and my dad prayed on the last day and said, "Lord, we know it can't always be the wonderful way it is now, but we thank You for the love we enjoy today." A month later, he experienced his heart attack; and in December, I said goodbye to my gentle friend and you put your arm around me and said, "I'm hurting with you!" and I cried and said, "I love you!"

And we invited my mother to spend six weeks with us during her recuperation period, and the three of us endured the loneliest Christmas of our lives as the empty chair and missing place setting reminded us of his red sweater and dominoes and apples and a stack of sophisticated books and a little dog named Benji who always sat on his lap.

But life went on. My mother staggered to get herself back together and couldn't, and lost 15 pounds and moved to California, and still ached for her missing friend. And more books were written and more honors arrived, and we became better known and our influence spread and we thanked God for what we had.

And our daughter went into adolescence, and this great authority on children knew he was inadequate and found himself asking God to help him with the awesome task of parenting, and He did; and we thanked Him for sharing His wisdom with us. And then a little dog named Siggie, who was sort of a dachshund, grew old and toothless and we had to let the vet do his thing, and a 15-year love affair between man and dog ended with a whimper. But a pup named Mindy showed up at the front door, and life went on.

Then a series of films were produced in San Antonio, Texas, and our world turned upside down as we were thrust into the fishbowl and "Poke us in the Fanny" expanded in new directions, and life got busier and more hectic and time became more precious, and then someone invited us to a Marriage Encounter weekend where I sit at this moment.

So I ask you! Who's gonna take your place in my life? You have become me, and I have become you.

We are inseparable. I've now spent 46 percent of my life with you, and I can't even remember much of the first 54! Not one of the experiences I've listed can be comprehended by anyone but the woman who lived through them with me. Those days are gone, but their aroma lingers on in our minds. And with every event during these 21 years, our lives have become more intertwined—blending eventually into this incredible affection that I bear for you today.

Is it any wonder that I can read your face like a book when we are in a crowd? The slightest narrowing of your eyes speaks volumes to me about the thoughts that are running through your conscious experience. As you open Christmas presents, I know instantly if you like the color or style of the gift, because your feelings cannot be hidden from me.

I love you, S.M.D. (remember the monogrammed shirt)? I love the girl who believed in me before I believed in myself. I love the girl who never complained about huge school bills and books and hot apartments and rented junky furniture and no vacations and humble little Volkswagens. You have been *with* me—encouraging me, loving me and supporting me—since August 27, 1960. And the status you have given me in our home is beyond what I have deserved.

So why do I want to go on living? It's because I have you to take that journey with. Otherwise, why make the trip? The half-life that lies ahead promises to be tougher than the years behind us. It is in the nature of things that my mom will someday join my father and then she will be laid to rest beside him in Olathe, Kansas, overlooking a windswept hill from whence he walked with Benji and recorded a cassette tape for me describing the beauty of that spot. Then we'll have to say goodbye to your mom and dad. Gone will be the table games we played and the ping-pong and lawn darts and Joe's laughter and Alma's wonderful ham dinners and her underlined birthday cards and the little yellow house in Long Beach. Everything within me screams "No!" But my dad's final prayer is still valid—"We know it can't always be the way it is now." When that time comes, our childhoods will then be severed—cut off by the passing of the beloved parents who bore us.

What then, my sweet wife? To whom will I turn for solace and comfort? To whom can I say, "I'm hurting!" and know that I am understood in more than an abstract manner? To whom can I turn when the summer leaves begin to change colors and fall to the ground? How much I have enjoyed the springtime and the warmth of the summer sun. The flowers and the green grass and the blue sky and the clear streams have been savored to their fullest.

But alas, autumn is coming. Even now, I can feel a little nip in the air—and I try not to look at a distant, lone cloud that passes near the horizon. I must face the fact that winter lies ahead—with its ice and sleet and snow to pierce us through. But in this instance, winter will not be followed by springtime, except in the glory of the life to come. With whom, then, will I spend that final season of my life?

None but you, Shirls. The only joy of the future will be in experiencing it as we have the past 21 years—hand in hand with the one I love . . . a young miss named Shirley Deere, who gave me everything she had—including her heart.

Thank you, babe, for making this journey with me. Let's finish it—together!

Your Jim*

* From James Dobson, *Love Must Be Tough* (Dallas: Word Books, 1986). Used by permission.

LEARNING-
DISCUSSION
IDEAS

Are you reading this book alone? With your spouse? With your intended? With a study group? Whatever your situation, the following questions, agree/disagree statements, life situations and Bible study ideas will help you work with Dr. Dobson's views as he discusses 10 common misconceptions about romance, love and marriage. Equip yourself with a notebook, Bible and pen or pencil, and you are ready to work with these learning-discussion ideas.

ITEM 1

"Love at first sight" occurs between some people.

1. Do you agree or disagree with Dr. Dobson's view that "love at first sight" is physically and emotionally impossible? Can the kind of relationship described in Philippians exist in "love at first sight"? Why? Why not?

*Then make my joy complete by being like-
minded, having the same love, being one in
spirit and purpose (Phil. 2:2).*

2. Do you agree with Dr. Dobson that popular songs can distort a person's concept
   of love? What about films? TV? Maga-
   zines? Novels? How can you tell the difference between "falling in love with love"
   and developing a genuine love relationship with someone? What does a passage
   like the one below have to do with "true
   love" in a marriage?

*Therefore, as God's chosen people, holy and
dearly loved, clothe yourselves with com-
passion, kindness, humility, gentleness and
patience. Bear with each other and forgive
whatever grievances you may have against
one another. Forgive as the Lord forgave
you. And over all these virtues put on love,*

which binds them all together in perfect unity.
Let the peace of Christ rule in your hearts,
since as members of one body you were called
to peace (Col. 3:12-15).

3. Is selfishness involved in "love at first sight"? Why? Why not? How do the verses below inform your ideas about love and selfishness?

    Do nothing out of selfish ambition or vain
    conceit, but in humility consider others better
    than yourselves. Each of you should look not
    only to your own interests, but also to the in-
    terests of others (Phil. 2:3-4).

4. Reread the last two paragraphs in Dr. Dobson's discussion of "love at first sight" on pages 28-29. List some reasons that the words "time" and "grow" are important to real love. Read the following Scripture pas-

sage as well as other versions of it and note words and phrases that you feel are related to the idea of taking time to grow into love.

Love is patient, love is kind. It does not envy, it does not boast, it is not proud. It is not rude, it is not self-seeking, it is not easily angered, it keeps no record of wrongs. Love does not delight in evil but rejoices with the truth. It always protects, always trusts, always hopes, always perseveres (1 Cor. 13:4-7).

ITEM 2

It is easy to distinguish real love from infatuation.

1. Do you agree or disagree with Dr. Dobson that "the exhilaration of infatuation is *never a permanent condition*" (pages 29-30)? Is any relationship immune from ups and

downs? Is any situation permanent? Can anyone truthfully say, "I won't change"? Read the following Scripture passages and consider how they inform your answers.

I the LORD do not change. So you, 0 descendants of Jacob, are not destroyed (Mal. 3:6).

Jesus Christ is the same yesterday and today and forever (Heb. 13:8).

2. How can God's changelessness strengthen and give stability to a human relationship?

But the plans of the LORD stand firm forever, the purposes of his heart through all generations (Ps. 33:11).

3. Does the following statement by Dr. Dobson strike you as (1) unromantic, (2) puzzling, (3) false or (4) a solid base for marriage? "Stability [in marriage]

comes from this irrepressible determination to make a success of marriage and to
keep the flame aglow *regardless of the circumstances*" (page 32). Explain your response.
How do the following verses compare with
that statement?

*May the God who gives endurance and encour-
agement give you a spirit of unity among yourselves as you follow Christ Jesus (Rom. 15:5).*

*Therefore encourage one another and build
each other up, just as in fact you are doing
(1 Thess. 5:11).*

4. According to Dr. Dobson, what is the neces-
sary ingredient that must be added before
you can really determine whether a person is
experiencing infatuation or genuine love?
Proverbs 19:2 talks about the wisdom of taking time to think through any important

step when it says, "It is not good to have zeal without knowledge, nor to be hasty and miss the way." How can this apply to evaluating infatuation and real love? What are the unknowns?

ITEM 3

People who sincerely love each other will not fight and argue.

1. "Some marital conflict is as inevitable as the sunrise," says Dr. Dobson (page 35). What is the key to keeping the combat zone healthy? Read Dr. Dobson's comments about handling conflict well. For additional ideas, read the verses below:

> *A gentle answer turns away wrath, but a harsh word stirs up anger. . . . A hot-tempered man stirs up dissension, but a patient man calms a quarrel (Prov. 15:1,18).*

> *Starting a quarrel is like breaching a dam; so drop the matter before a dispute breaks out (Prov. 17:14).*

> *"In your anger do not sin": Do not let the sun go down while you are still angry, and do not give the devil a foothold (Eph. 4:26-27).*

2. True or false? Can a married couple argue and still obey the Bible's teaching in Ephesians 4:31?

> *Get rid of all bitterness, rage and anger, brawling and slander, along with every form of malice (Eph. 4:31).*

3. Discuss the difference between being angry at your spouse and being angry or hurt by the issue or the problem. Is it always possible to keep the two separated? What guides for constructive conflict can

you find in the following Scripture verses?
Read the verses in as many versions as possible and list three key ideas.

*If you keep on biting and devouring each
other, watch out or you will be destroyed by
each other (Gal. 5:15).*

*Above all, love each other deeply, because love
covers over a multitude of sins (1 Pet. 4:8).*

*Therefore confess your sins to each other and
pray for each other so that you may be
healed. The prayer of a righteous man is
powerful and effective (Jas. 5:16).*

4. If you are in a study group, ask volunteers
to role-play an argument that demon-
strates the principle: "Healthy conflict . . .
remains focused on the issue around which
the disagreement began" (page 38). For

each role-play, choose from the following three issues:

"I'm worried about all these bills."

"I get upset when I don't know you'll be home late for dinner."

"I was embarrassed by what you said at the party last night—I felt foolish."

After each role-play argument, take a few minutes for the entire group to evaluate: Did the argument stay on the issue, or did it become personal?

ITEM 4

God selects *one* particular person for each of us to marry, and He will guide us together.

1. How does God offer help for choosing a marriage partner? Before you decide on

your answer, read the following Scripture passages. Is the help described in these verses general or specific?

Call to me and I will answer you and tell you great and unsearchable things you do not know (Jer. 33:3).

Look to the LORD and his strength; seek his face always (1 Chron. 16:11).

Do not be anxious about anything, but in everything, by prayer and petition, with thanksgiving, present your requests to God (Phil. 4:6).

If any of you lacks wisdom, he should ask God, who gives generously to all without finding fault, and it will be given to him. But when he asks, he must believe and not doubt, because he who doubts is like a wave of the sea, blown and tossed by the wind. That man should not think he will receive anything from the Lord; he is a double-minded man, unstable in all he does (Jas. 1:5-8).

2. What does the Bible reveal about God's will for a Christian's choice of a marriage partner?

   Do not be yoked together with unbelievers. For what do righteousness and wickedness have in common? Or what fellowship can light have with darkness? (2 Cor. 6:14).

3. In your opinion, what is more important: that a prospective mate be a Christian or that he or she be mature, kind, patient and so on? Give reasons for your answer.

4. Dr. Dobson says, "Anyone who believes that God guarantees a successful marriage to

every Christian is in for a shock" (page 40). What do you feel he means by this statement? Do you agree or disagree?

ITEM 5

If a man and woman genuinely love each other, then hardships and troubles will have little or no effect on their relationship.

1. Do you agree or disagree with Dr. Dobson's belief that the emotional impact of trouble can be devastating even in a stable, loving marriage? Why? Give real-life evidence (which you have observed) to support your view.

2. What resources do Christian couples have to help them face trouble and work out problems? Which of the following Bible passages would give you the most

encouragement during times of trouble?
Why?

*Have I not commanded you? Be strong
and courageous. Do not be terrified; do not
be discouraged, for the LORD your God will
be with you wherever you go (Josh. 1:9).*

*From the LORD comes deliverance. May
your blessing be on your people (Ps. 3:8).*

*So then, just as you received Christ Jesus as
Lord, continue to live in him, rooted and
built up in him, strengthened in the faith as
you were taught, and overflowing with
thankfulness (Col. 2:6-7).*

*Be self-controlled and alert. Your enemy
the devil prowls around like a roaring lion
looking for someone to devour. Resist him,
standing firm in the faith, because you*

know that your brothers throughout the world are undergoing the same kind of sufferings. And the God of all grace, who called you to his eternal glory in Christ, after you have suffered a little while, will himself restore you and make you strong, firm and steadfast. To him be the power for ever and ever. Amen (1 Pet. 5:8-11).

3. Dr. Dobson speaks of a "wedge" (page 42) that trouble can drive between a distressed husband and wife (mother and father). Identify at least three principles given in the following Scripture passages that can help marriage partners reach out to each other in troubled times and avoid the "wedge of isolation."

   Dear children, let us not love with words or tongue but with actions and in truth (1 John 3:18).

Dear friends, let us love one another, for love comes from God. Everyone who loves has been born of God and knows God (1 John 4:7).

Therefore encourage one another and build each other up, just as in fact you are doing (1 Thess. 5:11).

Each of you should look not only to your own interests, but also to the interests of others (Phil. 2:4).

4. List ways to protect love from the pain and trauma of trouble. From the following Scripture verses, choose ways to protect and strengthen love, even when things are rough:

Carry each other's burdens, and in this way you will fulfill the law of Christ (Gal. 6:2).

*Rejoice with those who rejoice; mourn with
those who mourn (Rom. 12:15).*

*Finally, all of you, live in harmony with one
another; be sympathetic, love as brothers, be
compassionate and humble. Do not repay evil
with evil or insult with insult, but with blessing, because to this you were called so that you
may inherit a blessing (1 Pet. 3:8-9).*

Which of these ways do you need to work on in
your marriage? Which will require the most
change in you?

ITEM 6

**It is better to marry the wrong
person than to remain single and lonely
throughout life.**

1. Dr. Dobson says, "It is [usually] less painful
   to be searching for an end to loneliness

than to be embroiled in the emotional turmoil of a bad marriage" (page 43). Do you agree or disagree? Why?

2. Do statements made in the following verses favor loneliness or marriage to a "wrong person"? Explain your answer.

Better a meal of vegetables where there is love than a fattened calf with hatred (Prov. 15:17).

Better a dry crust with peace and quiet than a house full of feasting, with strife (Prov. 17:1).

Better one handful with tranquility than two handfuls with toil and chasing after the wind (Eccles. 4:6).

3. List five constructive suggestions for ways a man can combat loneliness. Also list five specific ways a lonely woman can fill her life with meaningful activities. List your

ideas under such headings as "personal enrichment," "caring about others," "discovering new things," "spiritual growth."

4. In 1 Corinthians 7:8-9, the apostle Paul encourages Christians to remain single, if possible: "Now to the unmarried and the widows I say: It is good for them to stay unmarried, as I am. But if they cannot control themselves, they should marry, for it is better to marry than to burn with passion." What are some spiritual advantages unmarried people enjoy?

ITEM 7

It is not harmful or wrong to have sexual intercourse before marriage if the couple has a meaningful relationship.

1. Discuss specific ways the entertainment industry and other media communicate

the view that premarital intercourse is acceptable between any two people who consent.

2. Dr. Dobson cites anthropological studies showing how all civilizations that move from a strict code for sexual conduct to wide open "sexual freedom" end in disaster. How can a society enforce a strict code of sexual conduct and still preserve the freedom of the individual?

3. Dr. Dobson writes, "When a nation is composed of millions of devoted, responsible family units, the entire society is stable, responsible and resilient" (page 53). Do you agree or disagree? How does our society match up to this?

4. Keep in mind that "fornication" is defined as sexual intercourse on the part

of unmarried persons. Then, using the following Bible references as resources, explain the biblical view of premarital intercourse.

For from within, out of men's hearts, come evil thoughts, sexual immorality, theft, murder, adultery (Mark 7:21).

The body is not meant for sexual immorality, but for the Lord, and the Lord for the body. By his power God raised the Lord from the dead, and he will raise us also. Do you not know that your bodies are members of Christ himself? Shall I then take the members of Christ and unite them with a prostitute? Never! Do you not know that he who unites himself with a prostitute is one with her in body? For it is said, "The two will become one flesh." But he who unites himself with the Lord is one with him in spirit. Flee from sexual immorality. All other sins a man commits are outside his body, but he who sins sexually sins against his own body. Do you not know that your body is a temple of the Holy Spirit, who is in you, whom you have received from God? You are not your own; you were bought at a price. Therefore honor God with your body (1 Cor. 6:13-20).

The acts of the sinful nature are obvious: sexual immorality, impurity and debauchery; idolatry and witchcraft; hatred, discord, jealousy, fits of rage, selfish ambition, dissensions, factions and envy; drunkenness, orgies, and the like. I warn you, as I did before, that those who live like this will not inherit the kingdom of God (Gal. 5:19-21).

But everything exposed by the light becomes visible (Eph. 5:13).

ITEM 8

If a couple is genuinely in love, that condition is permanent—lasting a lifetime.

1. Dr. Dobson states, "Love, even genuine love, is a fragile thing. . . . A marital relationship must be maintained and protected if it is to survive" (page 56). If you are married, identify and list three to five things you have experienced in your marriage that put a strain on your loving feelings. List three to five experiences that have definitely strengthened your love for your spouse. (If you are engaged, or dating on a steady basis, talk together about this and identify problems that could put a strain on a love relationship within marriage.)

2. Read 1 Corinthians 13:4-7 in as many versions as possible. From this Bible passage, write a prescription for strengthening love.

3. Quickly go through your activities of the past few days. Based on what you did, decide where your marriage rates on your value scale. Is it getting scraps and leftovers from your busy schedule, or are you treating your marriage as some thing of great worth? Make a to-do list for the next three days. Take into account your workload, demands of your family, and so on. Does your to-do list include times with your spouse? Will you give these times number-one priority? Why? Why not?

ITEM 9

A short courtship (six months or less) is best.

1. To think through the validity of this statement, use the questions, statements and discussion ideas for the statement "It is easy to distinguish real love from infatuation."

2. Dr. Dobson believes that six months is far too short a time for a courtship. In your opinion, how long should a courtship last? How long did yours last? Could you have used more time to find out more about each other?

3. Is it possible for a courtship to be *too long*? Why?

4. If you are married, what did you learn about the personality and character of your mate after becoming husband and wife?

ITEM 10

Teenagers are more capable of genuine love than are older people.

1. Genuine love demands care for the other person, commitment to the other person, giving unselfishly of yourself. Why can

these be difficult demands for teenagers to meet?

2. Compare Dr. Dobson's anniversary note to his wife (pages 63-65) with Ephesians 5:28-33. What does the Ephesians passage have to say about being committed to one another? When you are committed to someone else, how do you feel? What do you say and do?

In this same way, husbands ought to love their wives as their own bodies. He who loves his wife loves himself. After all, no one ever hated his own body, but he feeds and cares for it, just as Christ does the church—for we are members of his body. "For this reason a man will leave his father and mother and be united to his wife, and the two will become one flesh." This is a profound mystery—but I am talking about Christ and the church.

However, each one of you also must love his wife as he loves himself, and the wife must respect her husband (Eph. 5:28-33).

3. Read Genesis 2:24: "For this reason a man will leave his father and mother and be united to his wife, and they will become one flesh." What does it mean to become "one flesh"? List specific ways you and your spouse are one flesh.

ABOUT THE
AUTHOR

DR. JAMES DOBSON is the founder and president of Family Talk, a nonprofit organization that produces his radio program, *Family Talk with Dr. James Dobson*. He is the author of numerous best-selling books dedicated to the preservation of the family, including *The New Dare to Discipline; Love for a Lifetime; Life on the Edge; The New Strong-Willed Child; When God Doesn't Make Sense; Bringing Up Boys; Marriage Under Fire*; and, most recently, *Bringing Up Girls*.

Dr. Dobson served on the faculty of the University of Southern California School of Medicine for 14 years and on the attending staff of Children's Hospital of Los Angeles for 17 years. He has been active in governmental affairs and has advised three U.S. presidents on family matters. He earned his Ph.D. from the University of Southern California (1967) in the field of child development. He holds 17 honorary doctoral degrees

and was inducted in 2008 into The Nation
Radio Hall of Fame.

Dr. Dobson is married to Shirley, and
they have two grown children, Danae and
Ryan, and one grandchild. The Dobsons re-
side in Colorado Springs, Colorado.